DISCARD

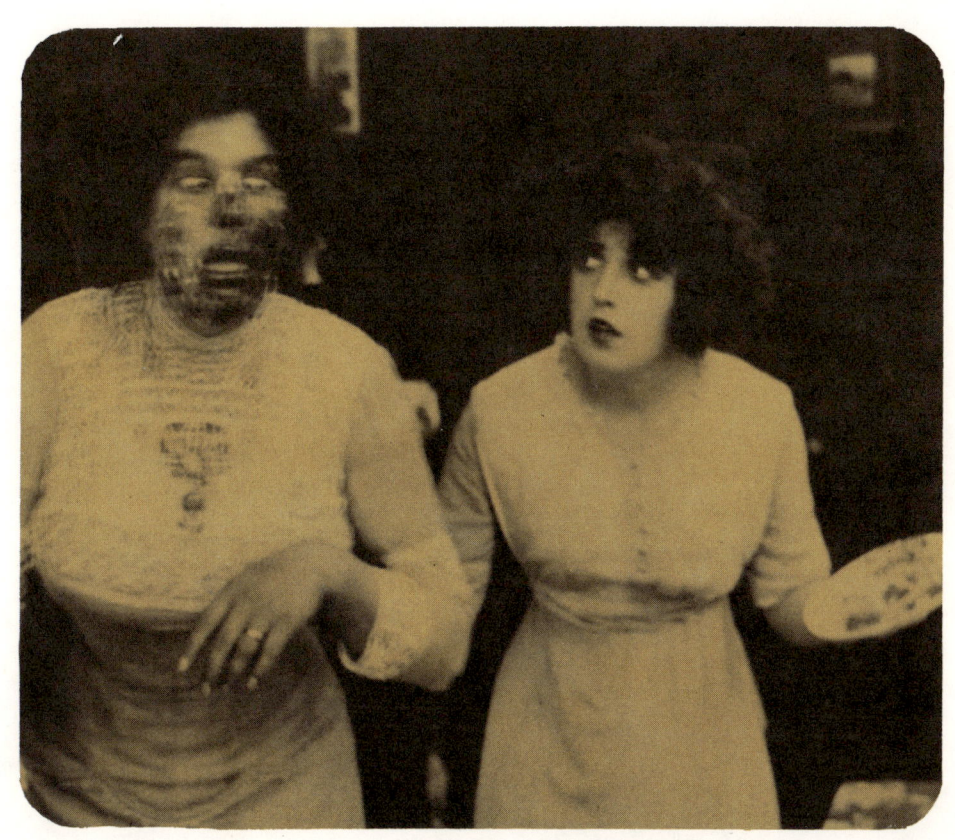

WHO THREW THAT PIE?

*For Dr. Annie Laurie Haston, Arcata, California,
film buff extraordinaire*

•

*The film stills for this book are from
The Museum of Modern Art Film Stills Archive, New York City.*

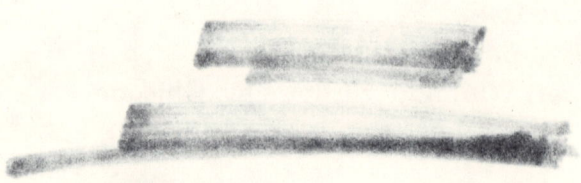

Library of Congress Cataloging in Publication Data

Quackenbush, Robert M.
   Who threw that pie?

    SUMMARY: Text and illustrations trace the history of silent film comedy focusing on such stars as Charlie Chaplin and Ben Turpin.
    1. Comedy films—History and criticism—Juvenile literature. 2. Silent films—History and criticism—Juvenile literature. [1. Comedy films—History and criticism. 2. Silent films—History and criticism. 3. Motion pictures—History] I. Title.
PN1995.9.C55Q3   791.43'5   78-27047
ISBN 0-8075-9058-4

TEXT AND ILLUSTRATIONS COPYRIGHT © 1979 BY ROBERT QUACKENBUSH
PUBLISHED SIMULTANEOUSLY IN CANADA BY GENERAL PUBLISHING, LIMITED, TORONTO
PRINTED IN THE UNITED STATES OF AMERICA. ALL RIGHTS RESERVED.

Contents

The World's First Moving Picture Gag 7
The First Screen-projected Movies 8
Silent Movies for a Nickel 10
Georges Méliès Brings Magic to Film 13
John Bunny, the Screen's First Star Comedian 14
Mack Sennett and Keystone Madness 17
Who Threw That Pie? 20
More Pies and Mabel Normand 22
Ford Sterling and the Keystone Cops 24
Charlie Chaplin, the Funniest of Funny Men 27
Chester Conklin, Little Fishface 30
Ben Turpin—His Eyes Brought Him Fame 32
Buster Keaton and His Look of Glum Bewilderment 34
Harold Lloyd, the Man Who Was Fired by Sennett 37
Harry Langdon's Great Art 40
Laurel and Hardy, Two Fall Guys 42
Kids Are Funny, Too 44
The Talkies—Goodbye to the Silent Screen 47

The World's First Moving Picture Gag

How did movie comedy begin? With a sneeze! At least that's what many people believe.

Here's what happened. Less than a hundred years ago, in 1888, Thomas Edison and his assistant, William Dickson, invented a boxlike device they called the Kinetoscope. The Kinetoscope made use of the newly invented flexible film, which was replacing glass plates in photography.

When a penny was put in the Kinetoscope, a motor turned and unwound a loop of film in front of an electric light. The film was made up of a sequence of still pictures. They flickered past the light just fast enough to fool the eye into seeing motion. One viewer at a time could see actors performing scenes from plays or vaudeville skits, or champion boxers faking fights.

The world's first moving picture gag was also shown on Edison's Kinetoscope. The gag was a long, drawn-out, hilarious sneeze, performed by an actor named Fred Ott. Nobody thought Fred Ott's sneeze was the birth of movie comedy. But everyone chuckled.

Follow the pictures down each row to see Fred Ott, the world's first comic movie actor, struggling to hold back a sneeze.

The First Screen-projected Movies

Since the early 1800s, inventors had been looking for a way to make pictures move. By combining ideas of others, Edison was one of the first to succeed. But as soon as the Kinetoscope was invented, he lost interest in it. The idea of projecting moving pictures on a large screen for whole audiences to see did not appeal to him, and he was convinced that moving pictures would soon lose their novelty. Edison had his Kinetoscope patented, but only in the United States.

European inventors, once they understood the principles of Edison's machine, built theater projectors. Screen-projected movies, even though they had no sound, were immediately popular. By 1896 audiences in every major city in Europe and the United States were seeing these movies in theaters.

Screams greeted the showing of one famous early motion picture. It was a film only one minute long, made in France by Louis Lumière. When audiences saw *The Arrival of a Train,* they jumped from their seats, sure that the train on the screen was going to leap out and crush them.

Audiences soon became used to pictures moving across a screen. They wanted more thrills. The public created the demand for moving pictures, just as now.

An audience flees in terror as Lumière's train rushes toward them on the screen.

Silent Movies for a Nickel

At last, Thomas Edison saw the direction movies were taking. He turned again to motion pictures. An Edison company built the first studios in New York City and New Jersey, to make screen-projected movies.

The Edison Studio in New Jersey was like a big black box. The whole studio was designed to turn on a platform to face the sun throughout the day. Without strong sunlight, picture making was impossible.

Suddenly, movies were big business, and empty stores all over were equipped to show silent movies. The admission was five cents, or a nickel, and the theaters were soon called nickelodeons.

Many companies formed studios in the United States and Europe. Film after film was cranked out for the nickelodeons. These films were one or two reels in length, each reel lasting about ten minutes.

Studios were partitioned into sets. Cameras were lined up, one after the other, so that as many movies as possible could be made at one time. Audiences became familiar with the names of leading companies, such as Edison, Biograph, and Vitagraph.

For the first ten years of silent-movie making, French films were very popular, especially the films of Georges Méliès, the first great film storyteller.

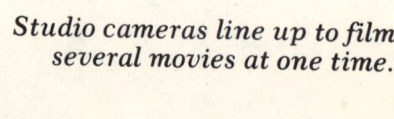

Studio cameras line up to film several movies at one time.

Georges Méliès Brings Magic to Film

Perhaps because Georges Méliès had once been a magician, he brought a special kind of magic to film. His motion pictures astonished and delighted moviegoers the world over. He invented or stumbled upon fast and slow motion, animation, double exposure, and many other trick techniques still used today.

Méliès's most famous film was *A Trip to the Moon*, a fantasy about the landing of a rocket ship on the moon. This was the first science fiction film ever made, but Méliès added a comic touch, too. As the rocket ship lands in the moon's eye, the moon cries.

Unfortunately, Méliès was no businessman. He sold his films instead of renting them. By 1914, he was being ruined by film pirates, who made copies of his movies and sold them illegally. Finally, with the coming of World War I in Europe, he burned what films he had and disappeared. Georges Méliès was not seen until 1925, when he was discovered selling newspapers on a Paris street.

A pianist plays lively music as an audience watches A Trip to the Moon, *made in 1902 by Georges Méliès.*

John Bunny, the Screen's First Star Comedian

During this early period of silent movies, few film companies felt they could survive by making comedies. Dramas were a sure thing and meant money. The comedy film was usually only a slapstick bit added to end a reel if there was unused film left.

The comedy filler was often a quick chase scene or a slapstick gag. One such gag showed a store owner letting down his window awning on a winter day and burying a poor customer in the snow that fell from the top of the awning.

Then in 1910, a forty-seven-year-old stage actor named John Bunny came to work for the Vitagraph Company. Bunny had been watching the growth of films, and he realized that the movies could show off his talent in a way the stage never could.

And Bunny was right! From 1910 until his death in 1915, he was a roly-poly, moonfaced clown who entertained movie fans with more than two hundred one- and two-reel silent comedies.

One of Bunny's films was *Her Hero,* a skit about a timid husband who stages a fake holdup to show his wife how brave he is. When the robbery turns out to be the real thing, the terrified husband collapses.

John Bunny was popular in every country where his films played. He was the first star comedian of the screen.

Mack Sennett and Keystone Madness

About the time when John Bunny began making films, a young actor named Mack Sennett came to work at the Biograph Company in New York.

Sennett didn't have much success as a film actor. But he soon found he could make money by writing and directing comedies. He decided to start his own studio, and he scraped together enough funds to begin. With a few other ambitious Biograph actors, among them Mabel Normand and Ford Sterling, he headed for California—more precisely, for Hollywood.

Hollywood was still just a drowsy sun-baked suburb of the city of Los Angeles, but life was soon to change as Sennett and other movie producers began to arrive. The Los Angeles area had a warm, sunny year-round climate, a variety of scenery, and low taxes—in short, just about all a movie company needed to turn out films from January to December without interruption.

In 1912, Sennett set up his Keystone studios in California, and Hollywood was never the same again. Suddenly Keystone madness was everywhere!

As head of Keystone, Mack Sennett was called "The Old Man" by his workers. He never liked the title, but he was stuck with it.

Next page: *Keystone madness invades Hollywood!*

Who Threw That Pie?

Who threw that pie? We could say that Mack Sennett did. He grabbed the empty pie shell of film comedy, filled it with delicious madcap laughs and thrills, and let the world have it!

And before Hollywood and the film industry knew what hit them, movie comedy was born. Sennett was impressed by the simple, tongue-in-cheek comedy chases from France, and he set to work with his studio crew to add slapstick and more obvious American-flavored humor. He slowed down the camera to make the action speed up, and he added outrageous touches and surprises—should someone casually close a front door, for example, a whole house might collapse.

If a lake was being drained or a balloon was being released near the studio, Sennett made up a story about it. Observers were often grabbed and used as extra actors. They might never have acted before, but they learned quickly from Sennett.

Mack Sennett himself appeared in many of the early Keystone comedies. In *Murphy's IOU* he played a stick-waving cop, while Murphy was played by comedian Fred Mace, a popular Keystone actor.

Comedian Fred Mace plays Murphy, who refuses to pay his bills, even though other Keystone actors, including Mack Sennett, do their best to persuade him.

More Pies and Mabel Normand

Early Keystone comedies were famous for pie-throwing. Legend has it that comedienne Mabel Normand threw the first pie. During a filming break, Mabel grabbed a cream pie someone was saving for lunch—and let it fly! A cameraman, always on the alert for any unexpected funny business, began cranking the camera and got the whole wild bit on film.

Audiences loved seeing people get pies in their faces. From then on, custard pies were always kept on hand in the Keystone studios, ready to throw at any time. Daily orders for the pies were placed with a local bakery. Soon the baker closed his shop to the public and made thousands of pies, only for Sennett. The pies all had a special filling, guaranteed to be sloppy.

Mabel Normand, the woman who made the custard pie famous, became the silent screen's greatest comedienne. She appeared in a long series of Mabel films, such as *Mabel's Awful Mistake* and *Mabel's Last Prank*. She was adored by millions.

And sometimes Mabel got a pie thrown in her face, too. In *A Muddy Romance*, Mabel's boyfriend came to the house with a pie he intended to throw at someone else. Poor Mabel stuck her head out the window at the wrong moment, and whammo!

Mabel Normand gets a faceful of pie in A Muddy Romance, *made in 1913.*

Ford Sterling and the Keystone Cops

The Keystone Cops were the real trademark of the Keystone films. These zany policemen were forever riding around in junky jalopies, chasing someone. Their old cars stalled on cliffs or in front of freight trains, and sometimes they fell completely apart, for no reason at all. Nearly every major comedian of the silent film era had his start on this famous police force.

Tuft-bearded Ford Sterling, a top Sennett comic, was the first chief of the Keystone Cops. Sterling was a former circus clown, and using his clown training, he fell, slipped, and skidded in comedy after comedy. He was also a talented actor who was able to put great feeling in his comic portrayals, bringing forth sympathy and affection from audiences.

As Sterling's popularity grew, he became dissatisfied and wanted more money. Early in 1914, he left the Keystone studios for another film company and better pay.

Just before Sterling left Keystone, Sennett was forced to look around for someone else to replace him. He remembered seeing a young actor in a touring English music hall troupe and sent for him. The actor's name was Charlie Chaplin.

Ford Sterling is ever ready to capture a villain, even though he and his fellow policemen have had an unfortunate collision with two trolley cars.

Charlie Chaplin, the Funniest of Funny Men

When Charlie Chaplin came to Keystone he soon developed the screen character of a hungry, shuffling little tramp who wore gloves and carried a cane.

Children discovered Chaplin first. They would come home from spending fifteen cents at movie theaters and tell their parents about the funniest of funny men. They would describe Charlie Chaplin's baggy pants and his bowler hat, and they would imitate the way he waddled when he walked. Their parents were finally persuaded to see him.

And soon adults, too, were in love with the little tramp. From all over the world, letters poured into the Keystone studios asking about him. In one year, Chaplin became the biggest male star in Hollywood.

Eventually, Chaplin's wage demands became so huge that neither Keystone nor any other studio could afford him. So he and three other famous Hollywood people—Mary Pickford, Douglas Fairbanks, Sr., and D. W. Griffith—formed their own studio.

From the beginning of Chaplin's film career, he wrote and directed most of his pictures. Today, his films are still being shown to new generations of fans.

One of Chaplin's most unforgettable films is *The Gold Rush*, made in 1925. In this movie, the little tramp is so hungry that he eats his own shoe.

Children were Charlie Chaplin's first fans.

Next page: *Charlie Chaplin dives into a meal of his own shoe, a prop made of licorice for a classic scene in* The Gold Rush.

Chester Conklin, Little Fishface

Chester Conklin was a Keystone actor who had played opposite Charlie Chaplin in many comedies, and who could have left with him. But Conklin chose to stay with the Keystone studios, and he gradually became one of Mack Sennett's most dependable performers.

With an oversized bush moustache and prominent eyes, Conklin was soon known as Fishface. In comedy after comedy, he played a pop-eyed character who was a bumbling know-it-all or the butt of practical jokes.

Chester Conklin is still best remembered today as Walrus, the little comic who made life miserable for everyone. Even babies were not immune to his wicked mischief, for Walrus would snatch lollipops right out of their hands!

Because he was a former circus clown, peanut-sized Conklin was ideally prepared for the life of a Keystone comedian. He was called upon to perform many dangerous stunts. During filming of *The Cannon Ball* he was suddenly blown sky-high by the early and unexpected explosion of a water tank. His keen sense of timing and confidence saved him and added a new twist to the film. In a career that spanned forty-eight years, Chester Conklin's only injury occurred when he damaged his knee at a charity baseball game.

Chester Conklin is nearly buried by a pile of bricks in Dizzy Heights and Daring Hearts, *made in 1916.*

Ben Turpin—His Eyes Brought Him Fame

One of the last comedy stars launched by Sennett at Keystone Studios was cross-eyed Ben Turpin.

Turpin's crossed eyes were the key to his successful comic performance. His vision spoiled his pie-throwing aim so that innocent bystanders were always being splattered. When he played a motorman he naturally could not help putting his foot in the face of a passenger boarding his streetcar.

Ben Turpin was at ease with the most ridiculous plot. In *She Loved Him Plenty* he played a clerk in a pawnshop. The clerk began the morning by calmly and efficiently burning and wetting down a pile of clothes, then putting a sign in the shop window that said "Fire Sale."

No one knew how Ben Turpin's eyes became crossed. The most convincing story is that he turned his eyes in so many times during one of his early stage acts that they became permanently crossed. Needless to say, Turpin was forever worrying that his eyes would become uncrossed, thus ruining his film career. He even had them insured by that famous company Lloyd's of London.

In Asleep at the Switch, *made in 1923, cross-eyed Ben Turpin plays a motorman who unwittingly steps in a passenger's face.*

Buster Keaton and His Look of Glum Bewilderment

Another successful comedian was Buster Keaton, who worked at Paramount Studios. Keaton, a well-known vaudeville actor, had been in the entertainment business almost from birth. Like Chaplin's formula for film comedy, Keaton's was simple—the small man against the big world. Never smiling, the stone-faced comic usually portrayed a character so absorbed in solving one difficulty that he missed a more important problem.

In *The General*, Keaton plays the engineer of a Civil War train who is so busy chopping wood that he fails to notice the train is passing through enemy lines. If Keaton is out rowing, the boat sinks; if he is boiling an egg, he uses a pot big enough for a hundred. In *Steamboat Bill, Jr.*, an entire hospital is blown away, leaving Keaton sitting in bed. Whatever the situation, Keaton confronts it wearing the same hat and the same look of glum bewilderment.

Forever a craftsman, Keaton worked hard to achieve special effects and would rarely use a double, or stuntman. While making *The Navigator*, he spent hours in a diving suit in the icy waters of Lake Tahoe. In *The Paleface*, he dropped eighty-five feet from a net, a feat reserved for professional stuntmen.

In The Navigator, *made in 1924, Buster Keaton is a diver who journeys to the bottom of the ocean, still wearing his hat.*

Harold Lloyd, the Man Who Was Fired by Sennett

In the 1920s people could attend movies in newly built movie palaces, many with full orchestras, ushers with gold-braided uniforms, and admission prices as high as two dollars. It was a golden age for comedy. Nearly one-third of the films shown were comic shorts.

Mack Sennett still produced the most comedies and discovered the most talent. But even Sennett could make a mistake, as when he fired a fifty-dollar-a-week comedian who wore glasses. Sennett didn't think the man was funny, but that same comedian, Harold Lloyd, went on to earn over thirty million dollars.

Harold Lloyd played a wishy-washy Charlie Brown character. But Lloyd himself was a man who would take any risk. Like Buster Keaton, he never used a double. But Lloyd's antics were even more heart stopping than Keaton's, especially when you consider that Lloyd performed most of his stunts with only one good hand. The thumb and forefinger of his right hand had been blown off in a filming accident in 1919.

In the 1923 film *Safety Last,* Lloyd played a department store clerk who is always looking for new sales gimmicks. When you see a man dangling from the hands of a giant clock fourteen stories up, that actor is really Lloyd.

Harold Lloyd dangles from the hands of a clock atop a skyscraper in Safety Last.

Next page: *Lloyd is nearly trampled by customers in* Safety Last.

Harry Langdon's Great Art

Of all the comedians in the 1920s Harry Langdon was perhaps the greatest artist. Langdon began his entertainment career in vaudeville, traveling circuses, and musical comedies and then made his way to the Keystone studios in late 1923. In the twenty-three short comedies he made, he portrayed a sad-faced character who confronted every calamity with wide-eyed innocence and a blind faith that he would somehow survive all difficulties.

In *Feet of Mud*, Langdon found himself playing football against hulking opponents, when he really would have preferred to stay benched. In another film he played a lumberjack who dodges falling trees and is mistaken for a desperate criminal. He took the role in *His Marriage Vow* of a bridegroom who waits for his bride—you guessed it—at the wrong church. Once Langdon even played an infant!

Langdon's genius lay in his ability to capture childlike reactions. Unfortunately, his film career ended when he stopped making comic shorts and began writing, directing, and starring in his own full-length features. Audiences were not drawn to Langdon's longer movies. His real comic ability could no longer flourish, and he faded from the silent screen.

Harry Langdon plays a baby in **His New Mama**, *made in 1924.*

Laurel and Hardy, Two Fall Guys

Two of the most enduring comedians of the great days of movie comedy were Stan Laurel and Oliver Hardy, or Skinny and Fatty as they were called by their fans.

Before Laurel and Hardy formed a team, each had made many comedies separately—Oliver Hardy had even played the villain for a while. When the two began to work together, theaters filled with laughter.

While most two-man comic teams had one serious straight man and one naive, childlike fall guy, both Laurel and Hardy were fall guys. No one could decide who was funnier, skinny Laurel with his timid whining or pot-bellied Hardy with his blustery bossiness.

Audiences howled at the fabulous pie-throwing scene in *The Battle of the Century* and at the destruction of a string of automobiles in *Two Tars*. Who could resist laughing at the silliness of such a typical Laurel and Hardy situation as the one in *Wrong Again*? There the two try to hold up a legless piano—with a horse standing on top!

Today new generations of viewers are chuckling through television reruns of the famous Laurel and Hardy comedy shorts.

Laurel and Hardy strain to support a piano and a horse in Wrong Again, *made in 1929.*

Kids Are Funny, Too

There were child stars who were talented comics, too. Over two hundred films were made in the Our Gang series, comic shorts about the antics of a gang of kids. The original group of nine child actors had to be replaced over and over as the players grew up.

Our Gang shorts were first made by the Hal Roach Studios, which also produced the films of Harold Lloyd. A few of the child stars in the earlier Our Gang films were children of the film crew for Lloyd's films. Jackie Davis was the young brother of Lloyd's leading lady, and Mary Kornman the daughter of Lloyd's still photographer.

The characters in Our Gang were always up to something. One time, Chubby tried to propose marriage to his teacher, Miss Crabtree, and Alfalfa once got the seat of his pants blown out by the firecrackers he was carrying in his back pocket.

Even off camera, the gang was busy making mischief. Once the kids kept the prop man busy replacing pies intended for the pie-throwing scene in *Shivering Shakespeare*. It's impossible to build up a good supply of pies when the movie stars keep eating them!

Members of Our Gang eat pies as fast as the prop man can unpack them.

The Talkies—Goodbye to the Silent Screen

The era of silent motion pictures came to an abrupt end in 1927 when sound was introduced in Al Jolson's *The Jazz Singer.* Suddenly every moving picture studio wanted to make sound movies. Soon a unique form of entertainment, silent comedy, passed from the screen.

The sad fact was that only a few silent comedians could successfully use their voices. Hollywood turned to radio and the Broadway stage to find "talking" actors. The Marx Brothers—Groucho, Harpo, Chico, and Zeppo—were the first of this new crop of comedians. The brothers were followed by the great W. C. Fields, who tossed insults at his enemies in a scratchy drawl.

And so the days of Keystone laughs and thrills came to an end. Mack Sennett and many other movie pioneers ended their days poor and almost forgotten by the industry they had helped create. But luckily, many early films have been carefully preserved by museums and libraries. The enormous achievements of the pioneers of movie comedy live on. Happily for us, we can still watch a pie sail across the screen and splat in the face of a surprised victim.

In the Marx Brothers' film Animal Crackers, *made in 1930, Harpo and Chico rough up a guest at a party given by Margaret Dumont. She was Groucho's love-hate partner in most of the brothers' zany films.*

About Robert Quackenbush

Robert Quackenbush is the illustrator and author/illustrator of over eighty fiction and non-fiction books for children. Among the books he has written and illustrated are a number of biographies, which include the lives of the Wright Brothers, Henry Ford, and rocket pioneer Robert H. Goddard. These historical books led to the creation of *Who Threw That Pie? The Birth of Movie Comedy,* about the history of early motion pictures.

The subject has long been of interest to the author. He was born in Hollywood, spent his summers there as a child, and attended and graduated from the Art Center College of Design in the area. He is very familiar with the story of Hollywood and the birth of films and film comedy. He felt he could provide new material and a fresh look at the history of early film; a book that would not only include important museum stills, but also charcoal drawings inspired by film fragments and rare shots.

Mr. Quackenbush, who is also a painter, resides in New York City with his wife and young son. His work has been exhibited in leading U.S. museums, including the Whitney. In addition, he teaches painting, writing, and illustrating to adults and children at his gallery studio in Manhattan.